street smarts

poems by

devorah major

curbstone press

FIRST EDITION, 1996
Copyright © 1996 Devorah Major
All Rights Reserved

Printed in the U.S. on acid-free paper by BookCrafters
Cover design: Stephanie Church

Curbstone Press is a 501(c)(3) nonprofit literary arts
organization whose operations are supported in part
by private donations and by grants from ADCO
Foundation, Witter Bynner Foundation for Poetry,
Inc., Connecticut Commission on the Arts,
Connecticut Arts Endowment Fund, The Ford
Foundation, The Greater Hartford Arts Council,
Lannan Foundation, LEF Foundation, Lila Wallace-
Reader's Digest Literary Publishers Marketing
Development Program administered by the Council of
Literary Magazines and Presses, The Andrew W.
Mellon Foundation, National Endowment for the
Arts-Literature Program, and National Endowment
for the Arts International Projects Initiative.

Library of Congress Cataloging-in-Publication Data

Major, Devorah, 1952-
    Street smarts / by Devorah Major. — 1st ed.
        p.   cm.
    ISBN 1-880684-27-6
    1. Afro-Americans—Poetry.   II. Title.
    PS3563.A3915S77   1996
    811'—dc20   96-2124

published by
CURBSTONE PRESS   321 Jackson Street   Willimantic, CT 06226

contents

shine

have you ever seen somebody
walking down any street
strutting
clothes laying just so
picked out just the right colors
to set off their tone
taking the street
like they own it
like they think they something
like they think they special
like they going somewhere

just announcing it to the world
loud and sassy as you please

ever seen those people
that move like they just
two inches taller
or that much smarter
or something more
proud people
make you say
"you ain't no better than me"
make you pull up
and stick out your chest
strut your colors too
because you want them to know
that that's plenty fine
that they think they somebody
but they need to know
that you, why you plenty fine too
so you just polish up your aura
straighten out your back
and tell everybody

to put on they sunglasses
and watch you shine
yeah
ever seen somebody
like that
who think they something
important
just like you
yeah
someone
going somewhere
doing something
righteous
yeah
just like you
yeah
ever seen that

you
watching
them
watching
you
shine
shine
and shine on through

kapow

listen
to the buzz
humming
around words
ping
pow
zap
kapow
tat tat rat a tat tat

place your
ear against the ground
next to the ringing water pipes
still your sighs
breathe in silence
stand in waiting
around the syllables
zap
pow
ping kapow
zip tat rat tat tat rat ta tat tat

as you listen
an earthquake tremor
becomes a four hundred year fall
off the richter scale
into a cascade of automatic rifles
recycled saturday night specials
two-bit twenty-twos
playing to a dying house
kapow, zap, rat tat tat
bam, bam bam bam
and then the gasp,
whine

shudder
thud.

last night bullets
rang again
wild west
live on t.v.
news at eleven
popping hollow and thin.
gunfire explodes against the night
flashes like a blaring series
of freeway headlights
caught in your rear view mirror
squeezing blood into your brain.
they pop against night.

beruit some say.
it has become a metaphor
so much easier
to deal with than reality
down under, right over
there
the need not look at
inner city outer limits.

not simply a burst
a new years debacle
a fourth of july surrender
but a rhythm
a nightly beat of armaments
pointed at self
hip hop ranting rhythms
with a bass oozi coming in
and shaking windows
on the downbeat swing.

beruit some call it as a metaphor
only its home the blocks
where bloods sharpen
fewer and simpler words
fuck meaning fuck
chill reaching beyond iceboxes
and motherfucker meaning more than the dozens.

they play wild west at night
when dawn should be
caressed and assuaged;
when lovers should
turn and stoke each other's backs
enjoy the crevices
between thigh/groin/tongue/cheek;
when babies should suckle their mothers'
breast greedy with its butter fat
spitting out thin yellow sugar
to gurgle at the clouded moon;
when old people need only
listen to their knees and elbows
creak considering if getting up
is worth all the angle sharp pangs
of inevitable aging,
but instead
the night begins its symphony
ping pop zip click
pop pop double pop
zap
chchchchccch
bullets burst as bubblegum balloons
around our houses and our dreams.

again tonight, and again and again
and the news calls it
somewhere across the planet
somewhere you don't live

but its here in your city
in your country
on your turf

close to each day's dawning
bullets converse
against a soon to be gray sky.
they chatter amidst
the plasterboard walls
and every dawn
no matter what battles
have been fought and lost
every dawn
birds come and sing
perched in the wounded trees
kapow
pop pop
double pop zap
in silent surrender they roost
as the children
play wild wild west for real
pop pop double zing zap
kapow

fillmo'e street woman

she is a dark woman
treading water
in a life of hard choices.
wrong decisions
limited alternatives
stockpens are embedded
in her eyes and mouth.

once she knew she was beautiful.

if you look closely
you can still feel
the edges of the fire that burned
in her eyes, on her skin
in the way her back arched
across fillmo'e street corners.

she wore her nails
sculpted in red
in those days
when that street
when this street
was ours

she sat on a barstool
snapped her fingers
and hunched her shoulders
as smoke rose between
the bandstand and counter
and the scene
got hot and sultry
and the music
pressed out the doors
and down the street.

further down
she slid in at jacks
had another cigarette lit,
flashed her teeth, laughed
as the club spun tight
shoulder to shoulder
thick smoke and blaring saxophone.

then she checked in with minnie,
bought a pitcher of beer and half-way
listened to some crazy poets
chant a continent of promises
with congo drum and shakere
punctuating the rhythms
and a flute solo
bursting out over
the tastiest of love poems

maybe, maybe
she slipped into connies
for some curried goat and coconut bread
or sweated spices next door
as leonard pulled another
sweet potato pie
out the oven and poured
his brown-red biting sauce
over smoking tender ribs
telling stories
as she savored another mouthful
then, when the street was ours.

she can see those days.
she knows them.
she remembers
before, before
imported cheese

before brandy filled truffles
before double lattes
hand-made paper cards.

she sits on the iron rimmed
privately owned bench
to rest her feet
and take the pinch
out of her back.
she holds the bitter in her mouth
sometimes spits it out at passers-by,
with steel in her stare,
there on that bench
on that corner
on that block
on that street
that was ours, that was hers
that was taken, that we let go
that is lost, that was fillmo'e
when the streets held the people
and the musicians had names
and the rhythm was blues,
and the downbeat was jazz
and the color
was black and fierce
like her.

"i just want to
party all the time..."

paaaarrtty!
i'll take it any way it comes
just give me some
dance children, dance.
as loving with the loving
grinds bodies into the morning
andre tailors jeans
to just above the hip bone
and below the belly button.
keep those hips a turnin'

dance children, dance

party world visions
madman distortions
drug rainbows
with empty buckets
at their end
up, down, all around
fast, slow, but low get low.

blisters grow
from finger popping
rhinestones and skin
blue jeans and musk
ropes tossed out to catch
anything that swims
or flies, or drowns.

dance children, dance.

summer becomes speeded
loud brass, moist jeweled
labelle and sylvester
climb the walls. party!
zebra comes and goes.
party! death jails swell.
paaarrrttttyy!

claudine is a hero.
cleaver turns to fool.
tyrone guyton is forgotten.
what spins around goes.
we spin in circles
real is not
fucking is truth

dance children, dance.

and summer leaves us
drained, thick tongued
quieted.
paarty.
it's a new year.
paaarrrty.

dance children, dance.

mixed breed

i speak for the impure
the cross-bred
the other than
the coloreds.
marked by our cast
defined by our tint
feared for our spirit.
we were not first,
but we still hold
the mother of kilimanjaro
in our blood, and we endure.

auburn, cinnamon, copper
cafe au lait, ginger, dun
we have no one continent
but we claim them all.

amber, ecru, gold
olive, dusky, shaded
this is for the tribe
that cannot be counted
on the fingers of one hand.
for those who have no single land
and can claim no aboriginal homestead,
the impure
the cross-bred
the other than.

the passion of exploration
the profits of war
the bounty of rape
the solace of love
the pus of denial.
we are repudiated by all

even, at times, ourselves
as the something else
and the something more
and the not really
and the never enough.
the ones you hate
the ones you love
the ones with whom
you have warred for eons
the ones who make no treaties.

call us arab
our noses, hair and skin chant africa
our noses, skin, and hair resonate caucus mountains
our hair, skin, and noses intimate india
call us arab

call us indian
our breasts, feet, and cheeks sing mongols
our breasts, feet, cheeks, spit aryan
our breast, feet, cheeks, remember ethiopia
call us indian

call us creole
our hips, waist, jaw swings of frenchness
our hips, waist, jaw bite of choctaw
our hips, waist, jaw speak of fulani
call us creole

puerto rican in new york
pakistani in tehran
algerian in paris
bengali in hong kong
call us colored
not you
one of them
an other

no tribe
no homeland
no anchor
no bond.

a human breed,
bleeding red
crying salt
showing bruises
revealing the veins
of all our ancestry.

call us nectarines
juice full, sweet and firm
our pit, large and hard
like our history
like our roots.
call us sister
call us brother
call us yours
or don't.
call us spick
call us wet back
call us kaffir
call us dog
call us cockroach
call us iguana of the millennium
call us survival
or don't.

turn away, try to forget
scorn the part of you we are not
deny the part of you we are
see our laughter
let it haunt you.
call us tomorrow,
that is our name.

you have no choice
everywhere you turn
we are mixed up with you.
so call us, call us
what you will
call us how you may.
then look in the mirror
and hear our ferverent answer.

altering anatomy

lover
why have i become enemy?
why do you not protect me?
why do you call me woman
only if i have cut off
my nectar-full blossom
and have no sentry
to welcome you to my valleys?

help-mate
why would you demand that i
show you my channel sewn closed
sealing tight the mouth of creation
so that even my monthly blood
becomes putrid and unused eggs fester
like the freedom lying
wounded in my shackled womb?

yes, i am woman.
you were born of my kind.
why does that make me enemy?
why do you beat, why do you rape,
why do you seek to disfigure me
if i will not mutilate myself
if i speak too loudly
walk to brazenly
drink too raucously
from the river of life?

yes, it is true that
i have given birth to more
than the dreams of men.
it is true
that of root and leaf,

water and candle
i can make a brew
that will make you love me
even more.
but i do not trade in petty magic,
trick of witches, fakir's chant.
i make simple teas
shaped by the way i
pick the stems,
sort the seeds,
draw the water,
fill the cup.

and if you cry when you touch me
it is not a sadness i give you
but a memory of another killing,
a different death of woman,
an ancient fear of your own difference.
it is true, that i am woman.
you then should be my complement.

look at me whole and unnaked, unveiled.
standing before you shamelessly.
offering nothing, but my scent
majestic, unbroken.

see too, the blade
i hold between my fingertips.
with its edge
i can pit a date
slice a breadfruit
castrate a bull.
it was not meant to pierce my flesh
or to cut out your heart.
but it can, my husband
but it can.

rape as it relates to incest

(dedicated to the boy who accidentally raped his mother
and his friends who shared the moment.)

hey, manchild/boy so young/so strong
when you took her/tore into her middle
when your hand pressed against her mouth
and she bit blood and hate
when you pulled aside her cotton skirts
jammed into her iron tensed birthway
as you twisted her womb
as she beat your back
as she cried/as she begged
as you came in thick globs of cream
spread them around her fertileness
how could you forget that in africa/times
she was of an age that would have made her your
sister/sister you would have called her name
as together you danced the harvest festival.

you, manchild/boy/struggling against the times
bent from the storm
eyes blindfolded with clouds of pain and madness
when you grabbed her from behind
when she feebly clawed against your
muscled hands/when you scratched through layers of
mildew and cloth to that center
preserved for god since her husband passed
when she bled as she prayed
when you trembled inside her
how could you forget in long past africa/times
you would have called her grandmother
bowed as you entered her home as she
shared with you kola nuts and sweet tea.

manchild/boy as you threw the coat over her head
never having seen her lips move or eyes smile
as you spread sweat into her tears
thrust hard into her middle
as she bled and turned to acid your life juices
how could you forget that in once remembered africa/times
she would have been called mother
in africa/times it would have been your life.

when you rape
would be man/punching power into strange
women's orifices
it is always a family affair.

cracker jacks

"step on a line you break your mama's spine
step on a crack you break your mama's... "
what, tuff enough, engraved scowl,
fine scar across your eyebrow?
tight jeans, glazed eyes,
piled curses, spent daydreams
reeling in the sunlight
barely thirteen,
crack full
little girl
five dollar pebble in your pocket
ten dollar trick down the block.

"lady bug lady why do you roam?
your house is on fire and your children are home"

little girl,
if you were my little girl,
i would take your face between my hands;
i would hold your eyes with mine;
i would look for the drop the spark that was me,
when i fed you at my breast.
child, if you were my little girl,
i would remember
work my way down the cord to see
where it began to tear
so i could tie up each loose end,
feed your hunger with my love.

if you were my little girl,
if you were mine, child,
the rage would know no end.
and i would plead,
"if i did not listen to you then

let me listen to you now"
i would hold you under
one arm and running, carry you
to the ocean of our knowing.

i would not let them take you away.
i would not let you become the blade
of the smoke you embrace,
reel, pull and puff,
puff again and call it home
and sunshine.
"eeny meeny miney moe catch a... "
i would do all the wrong things
and maybe some of the right.

little girl, little girl
with your grown up habits
which eat smiles
and devour lifetimes;
i would take you home.
more than holding up a mirror
i would make a door
kicking, pulling, flying
i would get you through.

daughter if you saw what i see
when i look at you
"i'm a little acorn brown
laying on the cold cold ground
everybody steps on me
that is why I'm fractured, see..."

i see the benin bronze
almond queen mother eyes
braids sweeping the neck.
i see nzinga curtsying to the
portuguese before proclaiming

there would be no slavery here;
holding spear, shield, and musket
to enforce her point.
i see the old woman, la vieja,
the first one who bled this land
holding the spark as she held her breath
determining she and hers
i and i was gonna make it.
i see the pyramids
and i see cowrie shells
laying open in pairs.

pick a star name it for yourself.
child i would take you home
and knead away the pain,
knead away the yearning.
i would bring you home
and this time, this time
i would teach you,
as i have begun to learn,
how to remember what we felt like
when we were truly free.

"what we gonna do 'bout dem youth?"

dem don't know
dem don't see
dem do what dey see
dem do what dey know
dem don't know what dey do
dem don't see what dey eyes look through
dem eyes don't see what dey minds know
when dem gonna stop gettin' high and look
at what dey don't be seein' and see what dey don't be knowin'
and know what dey got inside?
when dem gonna stop lookin' like shiny magazine covers
slicked wet and smelling of ink dripped in white linen perfume?
when dem stop wantin' the gift wrappin' and start
wantin' the package?
when dem stop wantin' the package and
start wantin' to run the store?
when dem stop wantin' to be the storekeeper
stop wantin' to be alla time a buyer, a seller
a commercial of disposable lifestyles?

when dem gonna talk about breakin' kola nuts with Ogun?
when dem gonna squat and drink rum with Shango?
when dem gonna dance the night in Yemoja
and comb dey hair with ivory from Oshun
wrap dey limbs with cloth from Oya's leopard?
when dem gonna find dey power

take off the plastic dey mold onto their heads
dat seep into dey blood so dey forget dey mamas, forget dey
papas, forget deyselves?
when dey gonna stop banging dem hard heads
against dem electrified boxes of won't happen fantasy?

dem is de promise
dem is de genius
dem is de love and de life
but dem got cotton balls soaked with fragrant pods
stuffed inside dey ears and dem feet got a hold
to a body snatcher dats pullin' dem into a quicksand
of robots, death needles and greased monkeys reciting
computerized nursery rhymes.
dem see selling dey bodies as a privilege
dem sees sellin' dey sisters as a profession
dem sees the mama and thinks her nuthin'
but a locked up heart and a empty room of a future
dem sees the daddy and thinks him nuthin'
but a street walker with a drug blanket memory
full of nameless women droppin' they babies down an
endless well of forgetfulness
dem is de children
dem is de children of Oludumare
dem is not chickens to be sacrificed and eaten
dem is not de beating of a sacred white goat
slaughtered and fed to Obatala for justice
dem is touched by Orunmila
dem is de children of Africa
dem is not a Babylon holocaust
a meaningless rage
a self consuming fire of hate
dem is Ogun's shield
dem is Shango's spear
dem is Ochosi stalking the jungle of nightmares
finding the prey and severing the head of the monster
swift, silent, sure
dem is de beads
dem is de candles
dem is de love
dem is not a picture pasted on a billboard
telling dem how to fit in a box, die and be buried
at an early age gray and toothless

dem is de hope
dem is de dream
soon dem gonna take off dem glasses with the backwards lenses
soon dem gonna look in de mirror of dey days
and see demselves sitting with nature
balancing the planet on its head
soon dem gonna set the moon to spinning
and pull the earth into a righteous orbit
dem gonna see
dem is de today
dem is what's happening
dem is de promise of what will happen
dem gonna see
dem is de love
dem is de tomorrow
dem is de new
dem gonna look and do for demselves
dem gonna be de night
dem gonna be de stars
dem gonna see demselves
the new Africa
the life
dem gonna take the universe
and make it sing.

newscast

death is dropped
onto my plate each evening, pressed
between big game scores
and electronic weather report.

        abbreviated newsprint
        punctuated with glossy photos
        cut away to open graves.

large spiny mouthfuls
of my dead relatives
are stuffed between
my clenched teeth
and tight jaw.

tears run
from the corners
of my eyes.

they ask me
to eat my dead.
swallow them whole

        neat
        like a shot
        of two hundred year old bourbon
        distending my belly
        leaving no waste.

they ask me
to consume my dead
and maintain my peace
my place
each evening

the days counting
is brought out
skimmed across globe

platters of dried and delicate babies
mixed with brittle forgotten elders
next to tureens of impaled mothers.
those who only needed to eat
those who rotted from man made diseases
those who imploded because their bodies
simply refused to fight anymore.

a roster of those killed or wounded in battle
civilization's unavoidable causalities.
a portion of suffering piled high
presented with a flourish
cacophony of applause

now
open wide
chew

cut to commercial

but, i have been taught
about eating the dead.
that it is not to be done,
unless, it is the heart
for valor, the muscles
for strength, the soul
for forbearance, the mind
for history.

eating their expendable
their unneeded
their discarded,
the bones cracking beneath teeth

scratching holes into lungs,
this modern day cannibalism
is always painful.

so, i have begun
to feed on life.
watch the african honey bees
who move and nest
and move and nest
migrating across continents
gathering, building and stinging
all who dare to exploit
the sweetness of their honey.
i come, you see
from people
who have lived for eons
making peace with deadly bees
while harvesting their lush syrups.

yes, i have begun
to feed on life,
which tastes bitter
at times, and sticky
like melon juice
or sharp like tree bark.
feeding on life
studying bees
learning to sting
fashioning a stronger hive.

zamani

the old people say
it just keeps going on
chiming ripples
of a pond
you
me
they say you can't die
say it's just not that way

           say the seed you sow
           is the ground your children
           walk on forever
           say nothing is ever truly forgotten
           and no one is ever really gone

it's good to listen
to the old people
they have lived hard and long
have taught truth since before
time cracked a wedge between the sun
and spit full the moon

ice chips

(for v. "They always have money for dope,
but they never have money for art")

1.

a poster of benin bronzes corner torn
stapled on a paint chipped wall.
another weeping George Jackson's
death clipped over the door.
a tacked up calendar of the York's
political cinema delights.
a tattered rug faintly concealing
layers of spilt wine.
paperback books hollowing out
propping up shelves.
a mattress spread with indian cloth
cross legged a smudged mirror passed
back and forth
noses stung as ice air hits the brain
moves it toward anesthetized serenity.

2.
he unfolded the paper
eyed the crystals
saw ice prisms
smile licked a finger tip
rolled a crisp bill
pulled it up his flat wide nose
with a long pleasured snort
refolded the paper
tucked it inside an inside pocket
fingered a fifty dollar bill
eyed the sculpture around the room
ran his hand aimlessly across a carved
ebony damballah mask

wished the artist luck in
the creation business
adjusted his wide brim
softly swept out of the studio
going to look for some trim.

3.
For sale one small piece of artist
painted in blood across parchment
a simple love poem
for sale a small piece of scraped across canvas
layered in sweat and sunrises of wonder
for sale one song soft and low
custom made with love for you
for sale a dance woven around cycling pleasures
full of tears for you
for sale a creation
that will not blow away.

partying with the snow queen

you're running. hard. running for the rapid river white frost sting your skin numbing. cutting hard. running fast. up and down unpaved hills reaching again for the dry white coaster that takes you in a down rush and swoop over dreams turning quickly into impossibilities. running fast. running high. racing so fast you can't keep up but, you keep rushing all the time, running fast, faster, fastest, dead up short until your heart grabs and your watery eyelids are the heads of rusted nails spread on the edges of your face as you circle the room looking for something.

is it your mind, spread beneath the razor edges/split in columns of white jutting like icicles crowning your head? trapped in smoke blown from pebbles and pipes, turning your blood to ice?

riding that filly who's headstrong, but you know you can ride her. wild and cunt-sure, she raises her shanks, throws you to the dust, and poised above you becomes grey and then red against the sun as her hooves stomp your skull sending its pieces around the room while she leaps the walls, tosses her mane in arrogance and finds another rider. so you rise again, to race after that mare who gestates only wild horses and feeds only on life, on you running, running, running again.

what was it that you used to have? fast, cold, running, huffing your chest about to burst your head, light starting to float away and you, smiling like a commercially certified jock, fantasizing about some anonymous cheerleader pussy. getting stiff and ready for some deep hard strokes when she calls you to her bosom and you reach out to find that you are alone and limp. staring at yourself wedged between the crystals and misery as finally, for a moment, you would give anything you have to stop even if it's just for another moment. but she wont let you admit

to being tired. so you wander around looking for something and you keep thinking it's her. running lost. running hard. looking for the end of the maze. hoping for some shade, as the sun sits high and pulses as you dare to stare it head on look at it hanging fire in the sky. its colors shoot through your eyeballs sending spikes to the back of your skull becoming a sunburst of oranges then reds searing back into the brain. you sigh, as your pupils turn to milky white looking for something you know you lost resting underneath a sunburst
before a mirror
after a reflection
inside the snow queen.
there.

tones

she say she don't like me
say she don't like the color a my mama
say she don't like my pop cause he think he know it all
don't like my brother 'cause he think he fine
don't like my man 'cause he dumb enough to go for me
don't like my kids 'cause they look like me
she say she don't like me
don't like me
don't like me
don't like me
say she don't even have to know my name
to know she don't like me.

getting past it

i know the sometimes
when it be like your body
is covered with leeches
and the sad just be
sucking out all yr blood.

that's the time you got to
have courage and pull them off darlin'.
can't get scared none.
it's easy if you do it right.

now, if you just lift the edge and jerk
why you leave the whole head inside
and are bound to get
all kind of infections boiling up
making pus run all through your insides
it can make you crazy
start you towards a dying.

but if you just rub those
little buggers real
gentle with some thick grease
why just to be able to get a breath
and swallow some more blood
those leeches is gonna lift out
they sucking pincers
and soon as they do
why you can brush em off
easy as you do
a fruitfly.
and the red left behind
wont be nothing but a memory
by the time the sun breaks
over the next morning.

one way to answer the question

for me
sometimes
this poetry thang
aint nuthin but a big wad of gum
softening up in my mouth

tell you the truth
sometimes it don't be
nuthin but its bubble
rounded by my cheeks
burstin' out all hot air
sticky and pink
around my lips and nose

and sometimes
this poetry thang
aint nuthin
but the spit around
the flattened gum

and sometimes
it aint nuthin
but the thrown out wrapper

sometimes it
aint nuthin
at all
this poetry thang to me
aint nuthin
aint nuthin
like those people
aint nuthin who glower
at you and almost everybody else

cause of something they got
stuck up in they own belly

it aint nuthin but you
just standing there
tryin to make you
a little light
in the inside of this storm
we all livin in

this poetry thang to me
sometimes it aint nuthin
but some bits of paper
wrapping up words
some hieroglyphic pictures
i have to sort out

and sometimes
sometimes it be clear
like my daughter's smile
all in and out of her at the same time
all in and out of everybody
she touch with it

sometimes it be warm
like my son's branching hug
all full and reaching
an overgrown puppy crowded with love

i mean sometimes this poetry thang
it aint nuthin but
laughin true with you
bout somewhere you and me been
one sunny tilted day
even if we didn't go there
at the same time
in the same year.

y'know, like that day
when the city was crooked
and the hills was steep,
and alla sudden somebody i knew
somebody you knew, honked they horn
and gave you, gave me a ride up the crest
& over to the next side

sometimes
this poetry thang be like that
and sometimes it be like this.
like this big ol chunk of the world
that aint doin' like it should or could,
like this piece of shrapnel
cutting into my tongue
full of starving babies
and walking nightmares,
and sometimes it be like
this tiny sparkly sliver of me
looking at you out the corner of my eye
and sometimes it be just like you
this poetry thang
and sometimes this poetry thang
it just be for you
and sometimes it just be
with or without you or me
it just be
this poetry thang.

c.p. time or why you always got to wait for the show to start

some say we can't be on time.
don't respect
or even understand it.
never mind our polyrythms
hip swaying
finger popping.
time
they say
is a mystery to us
too dumb
they grumble
to even punch a clock. yes
flatly measured time eludes us
like a fish swimming through
our river soaked hands
but then again
the time we keep is colored
understood in the cadence of the heart.

take a party where we divide ourselves
some playing the warm-up team and others
gathering to become the stride and peak pack
while a final few are roll up the carpet crews
instead of all coming at the appointed hour
civilized
punctual
reliable
dinner at eight
don't be late
time.

most of us
use different calendars
starting thousands of years before
this christ defined millennium.
it is true we don't acknowledge time
in seconds and hours.
we don't rely on time
in weekends and sabbaticals.
we resist it when counted in less than moons
we caress it when remembered in more than centuries
we do not fear it and it does not jail us.

which is not to applaud being late
i mean after the party is over
you have missed it.
and when the curtain has dropped
the show done been and gone.
say when the tide is low
you've got to wait
for it to rise
before you sail.
but time is not
a capsule
a dose
a molecule
infinitely divisible
something that can fit around your wrist
or hang thin chained from a belt.

time
is blue and has an incredible sense of humor
it has false teeth and an iron stomach
if you shiver, it can smell like death
and you can dance through its sunrise
and arrive on time in its eternally sensual beat.

interracial

if there is one thing
i believe my mother and father
have never resolved
it is time
the downbeat
the six eight swing
the space that rocks
between bessie and carmen
it is the clock
the hour
the moment
my mother has swung in mingus
cried as the bass hummed to the ocean
my father flown with dolphy
and rested in ranges of miles
it was not the music that formed the schism
it was time
the way it passed and waited
what it felt like when it hung
still, sallow
how to pick it up and run
how to stride
to sustain
to hold the beat
of the moment
time
they did not agree on time
it was
a
cultural
difference.

the wall

finally, it is finished.
the last brick has been laid.
the mortar sun dried,
hard, impermeable.
it was a difficult job,
despite all your help.

i was a slow learner
played over long
with the stones
let the wet clay dry
on my knuckles.
took years to learn
how to use the trowel
to smooth, then score wet cement
to create a tighter block.

from you i learned
to stretch and lift
square after square.
moving to your pace
spoon and spread
bend and squat
fit and press,
creating shadow
in a world of sun.

on my own, at the foot
of a trellis
that faces the wall
i've planted bougainvillea.
i love the way its magenta petals
curl around its soft green leaves
growing thick, and all but covering

the ledge. transforming the wall
giving it purpose and depth.

i think, in spring
i may put in a magnolia tree
for blossom and scent
to recall for me
a hot atlanta summer
of sweat and healing.

still, whenever i look
past the branches
and through the vines
i shall see the wall
and remember we
who fashioned it.

treasure hunting

i know you're out there.
i can feel the pace
of your breath, sometimes
when i walk down these frayed,
fragmented streets.

sometimes, i catch a coat tail
as you turn the corner
our eyes pause and hold each other
before we light switch
click back into places.

where you rushing to
so fast that you can't
catch up with me?
why do we only meet in glimpses?

considerations

it is a misplaced confidence
that allows us to forget the ice age
mastodon freezer death, even as they
ground clover blossoms to sweet nectar
between flat broad teeth.
some petals were found undigested
in the stomachs
so quickly did the ice
flow over their breath.

still, when i find you early mornings
poised in half sleep, hard and distant
i pull myself moist cream towards you
who slide inside as nearing a welcomed
fire, blanketed in yawns of waking
and nothing is taken for granted.
sometimes i believe we, too,
help the sun to rise.

marginal news - october 1993

these few angolan snapshots
were taken more than two centuries
after angolan men and women
shoulder to shoulder
at each other's back
considering the children
defeated the portuguese

defeated the portuguese
who in homage to nzinga's leadership
who in recognition
of the throbbing angolan heart
were forced to hold back their
slave ships and trade for
generations in a commerce
that included only things

these few angolan snapshots
were taken years after the portuguese
returned whip, chain and gun
holding captive the land and the people
until once more angolans remembered themselves
and rose up and pressed the portuguese
once more back, back into the sea
leaving behind rusting machines
valleys of graveyards
and blood-stained agreements

these few angolan snapshots
are watermarked by salty tears and blood

click the child's stabbing scream curls
from the remains of her dripping
shrapnel filled groin as click
nearby men shoot guns and lay
land mines and waylay food
and siphon off medical supplies
killing the women and the children
and the old as well as each other

click the little boy just rocks and wails
an older boy of seven wraps the remains of
a blanket around his brother's paper thin shoulders
"my brother was not always blind,"
the child says holding his brother close.

click the mother rocks in answer
somewhere outside the teeming clinic
where she seeks if not a miracle at least
some water not pulled from a pitch black
river where dead bodies float like
lotus blossoms before sinking to the bottom
her eyes are dry and
confounded and deeply hurt
as she squats outside this sun baked building
where she seeks if not
a full meal at least some softened grain
for her children

click wide shot of this place
which bleeds at the telling
hell the reporter says again and again
hell must look and sound like this angola

click an angola remade by her sons
who have forgotten how to love their children
enough have forgotten how to love their mothers enough
to love their lives enough to love

their land enough to put down their weapons
and talk to each other
and share the wealth
and understand passion and forgiveness

click angolan snapshots click click click

men and dogs

took a while of looking & touching & tasting
the sweets & the sours the too much spice & the too little salt
took a while of standing up with & next to
& sometime even underneath
took a while of dodging & ducking
& counterattacking drop kicks
aimed at my center entering through my vagina
trying to compromise my womb
took a while of rolling through
too few good summers & too many rain clogged winters
took a while of opening my eyes so wide
they wiped the frowns off my forehead
& moved my nose joint into a balanced perspective
took a while of loving & being loved & angering & being angered
took a bunch of rejection & a pile of reconciliation
before i started to be able to see right off
when a man was really a man
or if he was just faking it
wearing manhood
like the latest cut of running shoe
like a fat wallet stuffed in a back pocket
like some sour sweat lining a tight clenched fist
took a while to see that they wasn't all the way men
who were buying into the gruff & take what i want when i want it
without regard to female living beings
that they wasn't all the way men
who was chained to always being in charge
relying on her obedience & obsequiousness
in response to his obstinacy & obdurateness
took a while to see man
undressed from the cliches & insecurities
of genitalia easily wounded & often compromised
took a while to be able to just reach out & know
that that one there be sure who he is

be true to his self
be full of the kindness
& the passion
be the soft & the sturdy
be the full & the open
be the real & the imagining
be growing more & more into being a man
like i be growing more & more into being a woman
took a while to understand
that while a dog sometimes takes hold
of a corner of a man's spirit
you wont never find no man
housed up in the heart-space of a dog

on being a poet

the yng man uses the side of his mouth
smoothly without stutter
t'call me an "older spoken word poet"
doesn't know much about us he says
but says he's heard that i'm worth a listen
one side of my head bows
blessed for the compliment
but the other side bristles at its edge
winces at the accent on old

when i look in the mirror
to see how the years have bathed me
i see my breasts still soft
rest roundly across my chest
and my hips while not as high as before
still circle full and firm over my
thighs which can turn around
themselves as easily
as they wrap around another

in fact these last few years
i've felt myself as getting younger
than i've been in a long time
finally learned how to lighten my step
finally smoothed the deep furrows off of my brow
and although i've plenty of road in back of me
the part in front looks to be at least as long
if not quite a bit longer
and older seems an odd turn of phrase
for this particular situation

my mother is only now becoming old
my father moving to understand its syllables
his uncle has begun to enscribe its circumference

i however haven't yet qualified for the title
of older poet but i'll be yr
been around the block more than once
or twice poet
i'll be yr paid some dues poet
i'll be yr walked some miles poet
but i aint ready say i aint ready say
i aint ready to lay my hand onto older
i aint ready say i aint ready to carry its sign

y'want to put me in a file drawer
give me a brand name don't call me older
call me prime call me choice
or just call by my name
and if you care to
listen to me swing

calling names or why i like it when he purrs and calls me baby

we need to reclaim out language
not as verb syntax conditional
not as distinct defined syllables
in a rhetoritician's catalogue
but as true language
as sonorus groups of words
whose meaning is carried
by their tone and cadance

all my life folks
around me have been called names
duchess, duke, spice, bake
and baby for the mens
and baby for the womens
and baby for the babies

so i got to say that every bit as much
as i like being a full grown woman
my sweetie can call me baby and make me smile
name me honey and find me sweet
say aint nuthin in a name
until it rolls off the tongue
and wraps itself around
your privates

and if it don't fit
why then its a curse to be rejected
throw salt over your left shoulder
and return the barb three times
without malice

but if it makes you warm
why it aint nuthin
but a kiss
to be enjoyed
and remembered
so right back at you
baby baby
i got his back
just like he got mine
got his back
and a whole lot more
baby baby baby baby baby
just like that
i be calling me some names

CURBSTONE PRESS, INC.

is a non-profit publishing house dedicated to literature that reflects a commitment to social change, with an emphasis on contemporary writing from Latin America and Latino communities in the United States. Curbstone presents writers who give voice to the unheard in a language that goes beyond denunciation to celebrate, honor and teach. Curbstone builds bridges between its writers and the public – from inner-city to rural areas, colleges to community centers, children to adults. Curbstone seeks out the highest aesthetic expression of the dedication to human rights and intercultural understanding: poetry, fiction, testimonies, photography.

This mission requires more than just producing books. It requires ensuring that as many people as possible know about these books and read them. To achieve this, a large portion of Curbstone's schedule is dedicated to arranging tours and programs for its authors, working with public school and university teachers to enrich curricula, reaching out to underserved audiences by donating books and conducting readings and community programs, and promoting discussion in the media. It is only through these combined efforts that literature can truly make a difference.

Curbstone Press, like all non-profit presses, depends on the support of individuals, foundations, and government agencies to bring you, the reader, works of literary merit and social significance which might not find a place in profit-driven publishing channels. Our sincere thanks to the many individuals who support this endeavor and to the following foundations and government agencies: ADCO Foundation, Witter Bynner Foundation for Poetry, Inc., Connecticut Commission on the Arts, Connecticut Arts Endowment Fund, Ford Foundation, Lannan Foundation, LEF Foundation, Lila Wallace-Reader's Digest Fund, The Andrew W. Mellon Foundation, National Endowment for the Arts, and The Plumsock Fund.

Please support Curbstone's efforts to present the diverse voices and views that make our culture richer. Tax-deductible donations can be made to Curbstone Press, 321 Jackson Street, Willimantic, CT 06226. phone: (203) 423-5110   e-mail: curbston@connix.com visit our WWW site at http://www.connix.com/~curbston/